Copyright 2023 © Soumaya Arbes Issa

All rights reserved. No part of this publication may be reproduced, distributed, or transmitted in any form or by any means, including photocopying, recording, mechanical or electronic, without the prior written permission in the writing of the author.
www.juniorguidance.com
Insta: @juniorguidance

This book is dedicated to our mu'allem, our beloved prophet Muhammad (peace be upon him). Also to the ones who instilled the love of the Prophet Muhammad (peace be upon him) in our hearts, who taught us about him, and encouraged us to follow his path.

To the followers of our beloved Prophet Muhammad (PBUH) no matter how old you are, when you read this book, imagine that you are the one writing this letter. Feel the love and connection to the Prophet Muhammad, and don't forget to send your Salawat and Salaams.

اللّهم صلِّ وسَلِّم وبارك عليه

Until we meet in Jannah
A letter to the Prophet Muhammad SAW

Written by Soumaya Arbes Issa   Illustrated by Tayyaba Tanvir

My dear, beloved prophet, Muhammad,
Until we meet in Jannah...
I will remember you in my prayers every day
And send my blessings and peace upon you night and day.

I will learn your hadith and read your seerah,
Knowing that this will help in the akhirah.

I will accept and follow your sunnah And thank Allah for being part of your ummah.

On the Day of Judgment I will look for You to ask for yor intercession,
I will seek you first at the sirat.
The bridge that we will cross to enter Jannah.

And if I don't find you there, I will seek you at the mizan
The scale that will be used to weigh our deeds in the hereafter.

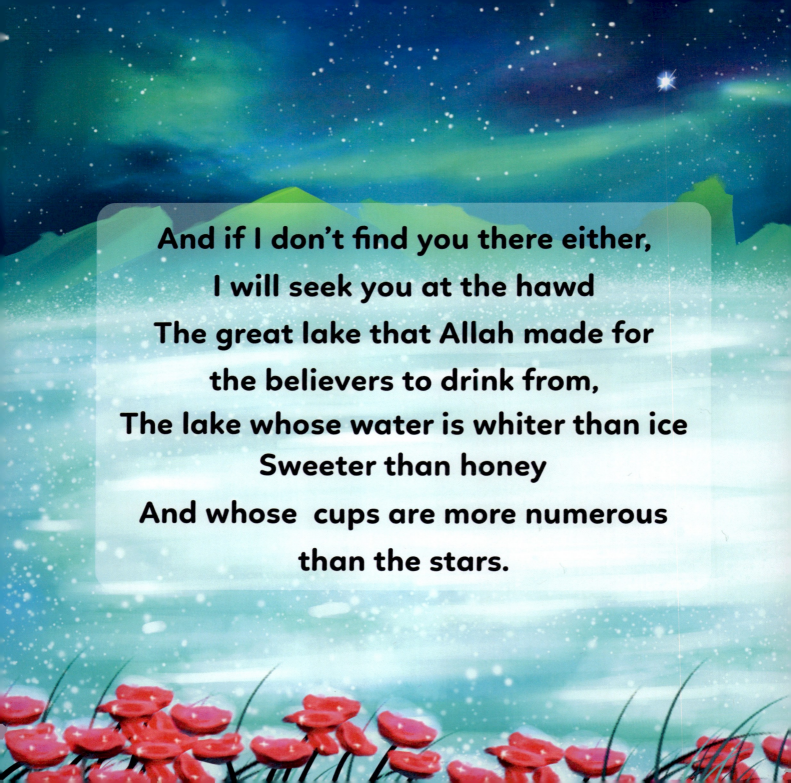

And if I don't find you there either,
I will seek you at the hawd
The great lake that Allah made for
the believers to drink from,
The lake whose water is whiter than ice
Sweeter than honey
And whose cups are more numerous
than the stars.

I can't wait to sit with you in Jannah and tell you how I dearly loved you and that you were my role model.

How I said 'Salam' to people that I didn't know, because you taught us to spread the salam between us.

How I smiled at people, because you taught us that smiling at your brother is an act of charity.

I will thank you for the knowledge you left for us,
For the manners you taught us,
For your guidance to become the best ummah Allah has sent.

Until then I don't want to stop dreaming about the day We will meet In Jannah.
Insha Allah!

And you, my friend, what will you tell the Prophet Muhammad when you see him in Jannah

Printed in France by Amazon
Brétigny-sur-Orge, FR